Designed by W. D. Stapelfeldt

DEARLY
BELOVED...

Written and compiled by
Peggy Yancy

PUBLISHED BY THE C. R. GIBSON COMPANY

*The compiler and the publisher gratefully acknowledge the
permission of the following publishers and copyright owners
for the use of the protected material indicated:*
Harper & Row, Publishers, for "Spirit of Love" by
Fulton J. Sheen, and "Marriage" by Edward Carpenter, both from
That Tremendous Love, edited by Fulton J. Sheen, copyright © 1967
by Fulton J. Sheen. Selections by Pearl Buck, Julius Gordon, John
Kendrick Bangs and Henry Ward Beecher from *The Treasure Chest.*
Doubleday & Company, Inc., for "My All for You" from *Poem Portraits*
by James J. Metcalfe, copyright 1948 by James J. Metcalfe.

DEARLY
BELOVED ...

My dearly beloved,
I come now to you ...
with love that will linger
a lifetime or two ...
Our tender journey
has only begun ...
we'll travel together,
forever, as one!

...WE ARE GATHERED TOGETHER HERE IN THE SIGHT OF GOD,

That there should exist one other person in the world towards whom all openness of exchange should establish itself, from whom there should be no concealment; whose body should be as dear to one, in every part, as one's own; with whom there should be no sense of mine or thine, in property or possession; into whose mind one's thoughts should naturally flow, as it were; to know whom and oneself there should be a spontaneous rebound of sympathy in all the joys and sorrows and experiences of life; such is perhaps one of the dearest wishes of the soul.

EDWARD CARPENTER

"This man and this woman. . ."
  (My heart breathes a sigh)
"This man and this woman. . ."
  Are now you and I!
All through each golden promise
  With rapture I'd cry:
"This man is my darling!
  This woman is I!"

AND
IN THE FACE
OF THIS COMPANY,
  TO JOIN TOGETHER
  THIS MAN AND
    THIS WOMAN
IN HOLY MATRIMONY…

...WHICH IS COMMENDED OF ST. PAUL TO BE HONORABLE AMONG ALL MEN

St. Paul has commended
   That lovers should wed
   After consulting
   The heart and the head.
I did . . .
   and "I DO!"
   Was what each of them said!

To love
is to place our
happiness in the
happiness of
another.

GOTTFRIED VON LEIBNITZ

AND THEREFORE
IS NOT BY ANY
TO BE ENTERED INTO
UNADVISEDLY
OR LIGHTLY…

Holy, Heavenly Father,
  How thankful is this heart
For your gracious guidance
  That led us from the start.

... BUT REVERENTLY,
DISCREETLY.

All true love
is grounded on
esteem.

BUCKINGHAM

Marriages do not endure
because people fall in love
with an ecstasy or a thrill,
loving the cake
only as long as it has
frosting on it.

FULTON J. SHEEN

ADVISEDLY,
AND IN THE FEAR
OF GOD...

...INTO THIS
HOLY ESTATE

This "holy estate" is more than a kiss. . .
More than a honeymoon. . .
More than sweet bliss. . .
This "holy estate" is a lifetime of love. . .
A lifetime of giving. . .
Of looking above. . .
This "holy estate" is one I wouldn't miss. . .
For God, in His wisdom, knew I needed this. . .

Surrender to God and to His will. . .
Surrender to life, and love it still. . .
Surrender to love and let it fill
Your life. Then let it spill.

THESE TWO PERSONS
COME NOW
TO BE JOINED . . .

There is no surprise
more magical
than the surprise
of being loved;
it is God's finger
on a man's shoulder.

CHARLES MORGAN

…IF ANY MAN CAN SHOW JUST CAUSE WHY THEY MAY NOT LAWFULLY

All paths lead to you
    Where'er I stray,
You are the evening star
    At the end of day.

All paths lead to you
    Hill-top or low,
You are the white birch
    In the sun's glow.

All paths lead to you
    Where'er I roam,
You are the lark-song
    Calling me home!

BLANCHE SHOEMAKER WAGSTAFF

The quiet surrounds me
And cradles me now. . .
Securely assuring
Each reverent vow. . .

BE JOINED
TOGETHER,
LET HIM NOW SPEAK,
OR ELSE HEREAFTER
FOREVER
HOLD HIS PEACE . . .

...WILT THOU
HAVE THIS WOMAN
TO BE THY
WEDDED WIFE,
TO LIVE TOGETHER
AFTER GOD'S
ORDINANCE,
IN THE HOLY

So long as we both shall live
All my love to you I'll give...

A good wife who can find?
She is far more precious than jewels.
The heart of her husband trusts in her,
and he will have no lack of gain.
She does him good, and not harm,
all the days of her life.
She opens her mouth with wisdom,
and the teaching of kindness
is on her tongue.
She looks well to the ways of her household,
and does not eat the bread of idleness.
Her children rise up and call her blessed;
her husband also, and he praises her:
"Many women have done excellently,
but you surpass them all."
Charm is deceitful, and beauty is vain,
but a woman who fears the Lord
is to be praised.
Give her of the fruit of her hands,
and let her works praise her in the gates.

PROVERBS 31:10-12, 26-31

ESTATE
OF MATRIMONY?

...WILT THOU
LOVE HER

Love is a proud and gentle thing,
   a better thing to own
Than all of the wide impossible stars
   over the heavens blown,
And the little gifts her hand gives
   are careless given or taken,
And though the whole great world break,
   the heart of her is not shaken. . .
Love is a viol in the wind,
   a viol never stilled.

And mine of all is the surest
   that ever time has willed. . .
And the things that love gives after
   shall be as they were before,
For life is only a small house. . .
   and love is an open door.

ORRICK JOHNS

It is the nature of love
to work in a thousand
different ways.

ST. TERESA

COMFORT HER,
HONOR AND
KEEP HER . . .

The heart
of him who truly loves
is a paradise on earth;
he has God in himself,
for God is love.

LAMENNAIS

... AND, FORSAKING ALL OTHERS, KEEP THEE ONLY UNTO HER, SO LONG AS YE BOTH SHALL LIVE ?

It is with life as with a play:
what matters is not how long it is,
but how good it is.

SENECA

Love is patient and kind;
love is not jealous or boastful;
it is not arrogant or rude.
Love does not insist on its own way;
it does not rejoice at wrong,
but rejoices in the right.
Love bears all things, believes
all things, hopes all things,
endures all things.
Love never ends; as for prophecies,
they will pass away; as for tongues,
they will cease; as for knowledge,
it will pass away.
. . . So faith, hope, love abide,
these three, but the greatest
of these is love.

I CORINTHIANS 13 : 4-8, 13

...WILT THOU HAVE THIS
WEDDED HUSBAND, TO
GOD'S ORDINANCE
OF MATRIMONY? WILT
COMFORT HIM
AND, FORSAKING ALL
ONLY UNTO

The highest happiness on
earth is in marriage. Every man who
is happily married is a successful
man even if he has failed
in everything else.

WILLIAM LYON PHELPS

MAN TO BE THY
LIVE TOGETHER AFTER
IN THE HOLY ESTATE
THOU LOVE HIM,
HONOR AND KEEP HIM,
OTHERS, KEEP THEE
HIM, SO LONG AS YE
BOTH SHALL LIVE ?

Love cannot be forced,
love cannot be coaxed and teased.
It comes out of heaven
unasked and unsought.

PEARL S. BUCK

Let us not love in word,
neither in tongue;
but in deed and truth.

I JOHN 3:18

How do I love thee? Let me count the ways.
I love thee to the depth and breadth and height
My soul can reach, when feeling out of sight
For the ends of Being and ideal Grace.
I love thee to the level of everyday's
Most quiet need, by sun and candle-light.
I love thee freely, as men strive for right;
I love thee purely, as they turn from praise.
I love thee with the passion put to use
In my old griefs, and with my childhood's faith.
I love thee with a love I seemed to lose
With my lost saints — I love thee with the breath,
Smiles, tears, of all my life! — and, if God choose,
I shall but love thee better after death.

ELIZABETH BARRETT BROWNING

... I TAKE THEE
TO BE MY
WEDDED WIFE,
TO HAVE AND TO HOLD,
FROM THIS DAY
FORWARD ...

And the Lord God said,
It is not good that the man
should be alone;
I will make him an help
meet for him.

GENESIS 2:18

...FOR BETTER,
FOR WORSE,
FOR RICHER,
FOR POORER,
IN SICKNESS AND
IN HEALTH,
TO LOVE AND

Love
is a circle, that
doth restless move
in the same sweet
eternity of
Love.

ROBERT HERRICK

Shall I compare thee to a summer's day?
Thou art more lovely and more temperate.
Rough winds do shake the darling buds of May,
And summer's lease hath all too short a date:
Sometimes too hot the eye of heaven shines,
And often is his gold complexion dimmed:
And every fair from fair sometime declines,
By chance, or nature's changing course, untrimmed:
But thy eternal summer shall not fade
Nor lose possession of that fair thou owest;
Nor shall Death brag thou wanderest in his shade
When in eternal lines to time thou growest.
So long as men can breathe or eyes can see
So long lives this, and this gives life to thee.

WILLIAM SHAKESPEARE

O CHERISH,
TILL DEATH
US DO PART…

...I TAKE THEE
TO BE MY
WEDDED HUSBAND,
TO HAVE AND
TO HOLD

I need so much the quiet of your love
    After the day's loud strife;
I need your calm all other things above
    After the stress of life.

I crave the haven that in your dear heart lies
    After all toil is done;
I need the starshine of your lovely eyes
    After the day's great sun.

CHARLES HANSON TOWNE

There is dew for the flow'ret;
And honey for the bee,
And bowers for the wild bird,
And love for you and me.

There are tears for the many
And pleasures for the few;
But let the world pass on, dear,
There's love for me and you.

THOMAS HOOD

FROM THIS DAY
FORWARD...

I am my beloved's,
and my beloved is mine...

SONG OF SOLOMON 6:3

...FOR BETTER,
FOR WORSE,
FOR RICHER,
FOR POORER,
IN SICKNESS
AND IN HEALTH,
TO LOVE

Love is not blind...
It sees more, not less.
But because it sees more,
It is willing to see less.

JULIUS GORDON

The kindest and the happiest pair
Will find occasion to forbear;
And something, every day they live,
To pity, and perhaps forgive.

WILLIAM COWPER

To everything there is a season,
and a time to every purpose under
the heaven; a time to love.

ECCLESIASTES 3:1

AND TO CHERISH,
TILL DEATH
US DO PART...

...WITH THIS RING
I THEE WED.

If you could know the part you play . . . In all
I try to be . . . You would begin to understand . . .
How much you mean to me . . . And you would
know that everything . . . I ever undertake . . .
Is not for my convenience but . . . For your
beloved sake . . . That I am happy only when . . .
I know that what I do . . . Will ultimately bring
about . . . Some happiness for you . . . I never
see the sun begin . . . Or end another day . . .
Without I say a silent prayer . . . To help you on
your way . . . You mean so much to me that I . . .
Must honestly confess . . . That everything
I ever do . . . is for your happiness.

JAMES J. METCALFE

AND WITH
ALL MY
WORLDLY GOODS
I THEE ENDOW…

Love never reasons, but profusely gives;
gives, like a thoughtless prodigal,
its all, and trembles then
lest it has done too little.

HANNAH MORE

... IN THE NAME
OF THE FATHER,
AND OF THE SON,
AND OF THE
HOLY GHOST.
AMEN.

Of all the music
that reached farthest into heaven,
it is the beating of
a loving heart.

HENRY WARD BEECHER

Joy is the happiness of love
. . . love aware of its own
inner happiness.
Pleasure comes from without,
but joy comes from within,
and it is, therefore,
within the reach of everyone
in the world.
For if there is sadness in our
hearts, it is because there
is not enough love.
But to be loved, we must
be lovable; to be lovable, we
must be good; to be good,
we must know Goodness, and
to know Goodness is to
love God, and neighbor, and
everybody in the world.

FULTON J. SHEEN

... INASMUCH AS
THIS MAN AND THIS
WOMAN HAVE,

I would give you flowers,
Golden, glad and gay...
And a bird of happiness
To brighten every day...
I would give you memories
That should be tucked away...
In some small corner of your heart
Where they, perchance, may stay...
I would give you tenderness
And love without delay...
All I own I offer you, forever,
Come what may...
I would give a prayer for you
That God shall fill your cup...
But one thing I would not give:
I would not give you up!

Love is the emblem of eternity:
it confounds all notions of time,
effaces all memory of a beginning,
all fear of an end.

MADAME DE STAEL

IN THE PRESENCE
OF GOD AND
THESE WITNESSES,
CONSENTED TOGETHER
TO BE JOINED IN
THE LAWFUL BONDS
OF MATRIMONY….

...AND THERETO
HAVE GIVEN
AND PLEDGED
THEIR TROTH

Do you ask what the birds say? The sparrow, the dove,
The linnet and thrush say, "I love and I love!"
In the winter they're silent. . . the wind is so strong;
What it says, I don't know, but it sings a loud song.
But green leaves, and blossoms, and sunny warm weather,
And singing, and loving. . . all come back together.
But the lark is so brimful of gladness and love,
The green fields below him, the blue sky above,
That he sings, and he sings, and for ever sings he. . .
"I love my Love, and my Love loves me!"

SAMUEL TAYLOR COLERIDGE

Love does not consist
in gazing at each other, but
in looking outward together
in the same direction.

ANTOINE DE SAINT-EXUPERY

EACH TO THE OTHER
AND HAVE
DECLARED THE SAME
BY GIVING
AND RECEIVING
A RING…

...I PRONOUNCE THAT

I wish I could remember the first day,
First hour, first moment of your meeting me,
If bright or dim the season, it might be
Summer or winter for aught I can say;
So unrecorded did it slip away,
So blind was I to see and to foresee,
So dull to mark the budding of my tree
That would not blossom yet for many a May.
If only I could recollect it, such
A day of days! I let it come and go
As traceless as a thaw of bygone snow;
It seemed to mean so little, meant so much;
If only now I could recall that touch,
First touch of hand in hand. . .
Did one but know!

CHRISTINA GEORGINA ROSSETTI

THEY ARE MAN
AND WIFE, IN THE
NAME OF THE FATHER,
AND OF THE SON,
AND OF THE
HOLY GHOST.
AMEN.

. . . This is now bone of my bones and flesh of my flesh. . .
Therefore shall a man leave his father and his mother,
and shall cleave unto his wife: and they shall be
one flesh.

GENESIS 2:23-24

...WHAT THEREFORE GOD HATH JOINED TOGETHER, LET NOT MAN PUT ASUNDER.

There's a bliss beyond all that the minstrel has told,
When two, that are link'd in one heavenly tie,
With heart never changing, and brow never cold,
Love on thro' all ills, and love on till they die.
One hour of all passion so sacred is worth
Whole ages of heartless and wandering bliss;
And oh! if there be an Elysium on earth,
It is this . . . it is this!

THOMAS MOORE

First time I saw you, I saw but you. . .
Next time I saw you, I saw God, too. . .
How shining now the moments
When your life comes in view
For love, alone, illumines
And the grace of God glows through!
Sustained am I and thankful
For God has touched my life,
As if with benediction,
And made of me your wife!

Love is, of course,
the supremely unaccountable joy. . .
Unhug your love if you would keep it
as sweet as its divine beginning. . .

SUSAN CLEGHORN

When I am old and have the time,
I shall sit down and write a rhyme
Or ring glad bells and shout with glee
Because my Darling married me!

THE LORD
BLESS YOU
AND KEEP YOU.
THE LORD MAKE
HIS FACE TO SHINE
UPON YOU AND BE
GRACIOUS UNTO YOU.
THE LORD LIFT UP HIS
COUNTENANCE UPON
YOU AND GIVE YOU
PEACE THROUGH
JESUS CHRIST
OUR LORD.
AMEN.